Eclectic Expressions

By Carmen Bouldin

Copyright © 2025 Carmen Bouldin

All rights reserved. No part of this publication may be reproduced, distributed, or transmitted in any form by any means, including photocopying, recording, or other electronic methods without the prior written permission of the author, except in the case of brief quotations embodied in reviews and certain other noncommercial uses permitted by copyright law. For permission requests, email the author at the email address below.

Carmen Bouldin
Email address: carmenbouldin@gmail.com
Website: www.thequotableraven.com

ISBN: 978-1-967407-04-0

Cover design: J. A. Smith

To my father who always encouraged me to write.

Table of Contents

Educate

10 100 School Days
12 Kindergarten, Kindergarten
14 We are Truly Winners
16 Senior Rap
18 Once Upon a Winter Rest

Esteem

22 The Memory Tree
24 My Brothers Three
26 February Gal
28 Go Put Your Lipstick On
30 My White Haired Angel
32 Memories with My Dad
34 Uncle Tony
36 The Giving Season

Embrace

40 The Restless Sea
42 Vows
44 Happy Anniversary
46 Discount Flowers

Enrich

50 The Unbudded Rose
52 Winding Through Life
54 Make it So
56 The Scarlet Path
58 A New Paradigm
60 Turning Fifty

Extend

64 50 by 50
66 Tristar Traveling
68 The Urban Playground
70 Whispering, Texting, Walking, &Talking
72 Traveling the Electronic Christmas Highway
74 Land of Enchantment
76 NYC Sounds
78 Minnesota: Land of 10,000 Lakes
80 This is West Virginia
82 Party on Wheels
84 Summer Escape to Firefly Cottage
86 The Watery Dance in Key Largo
88 Don't Skimp the Mint

Endure

92 Why did you leave me all alone?
94 The Unsettled Soul
96 The Seminal Sea
98 Shrill Cry for a Forlorn Love
100 Displaced
102 Connections

Exist

106 Ode to Coffee
108 Longing for Spring
110 Ode to Spring
112 Daisies
114 The Pink Gardenia
116 Fireflies
118 Will it be Fire, or will it be Ice?

Chapter One

Educate

100 School Days

100 School days...
A number larger than ones and tens we would say.

Oh, a number so big!
It even makes us dance a jig.

How much have we learned along the way?
Many colors like red, blue, green, and even gray.

100 words read by bright light.
100 words we recognize by sight.

Counting to 100 on the path we stayed.
How many ten frames is 100, Oops, we will save that for another grade.

100 CVC words such as c...a...r.
Sounding it right, makes us all shining stars.

Our teachers provided us all the tools for our brains.
Where we all have made lots of reading and math gains.

100 School days have passed,
Always practicing our writing with sky, fence, and grass.

100 School days smarter are we!
Dancing in celebration with utter glee.

100 School days...Not letting our teachers down.
Today, proudly wearing our 100 School days crown.

Kindergarten, Kindergarten

August, August, where did the time go?
Learning, and imagining every day to grow.

Segmenting and counting every single day.
Looking towards our bright futures along the way.

January, January, where did you run?
Reading about snow days and writing sentences for fun.

We celebrated famous cats with glee
On special days with teachers, we can agree.

May, May, here we are today,
Celebrating the Kindergarten Class in a big way.

Kindergarten, Kindergarten, where did you go?
We now cross the bridge to 1st Grade with our skills to show and smiles all a glow.

We are Truly Winners

The time has come,
The crowd is here,
We walk to the mat
While everyone cheers.
We have worked and cried
Now we face our fear:
Competition day
Without frustrating tears.

We're ready for the fight,
We can hit it clean.
Everyone is ready
To live our dream.
There is no looking back,
The time is right,
Doing our best
Using all our might.

You see, we know we can
Because we are a TEAM.
There are no individuals
On their own who scream.
Win or lose
Important may seem,
But if we give it our all
We have lived our dream.

We are truly winners
In everyone's thoughts
Because we finished it together
And together we brought
The most valued lesson
That could be sought.

Senior Rap

I know this is funny, but act your age.
Don't act your shoe size or your GPA.
This year went by so fast, the spring, summer, and fall.
So we're gonna' use this rap to explain it all.

The school year started out fine and dandy.
Driver's Ed was handin' out some smart candy.
You thought you were late, but you made it on the chimes,
Then the teacher said, Tuck in time!!!

Football had a great and exciting year,
In many opponents, they struck Wolverine fear.
The Basketball team was pretty ballin'.
They broke some ankles and saw their opponents fallin'.
The baseball team is doin' great.
They just beat the opposing tema four to eight.

The band was rockin' out with a nightmare Christmas.
All the other schools could never keep up with us.
Drama had cool plays and the excitement spread,
With California hillibillies and the night of those dead.
Boys' soccer is still goin' on,
They're 6-1-3 and still goin' strong.

This is the end, the time is near,
We wish you the best for your future years.
You got the best teachers; we think we're all that.
That's why we brought you this really cool rap.

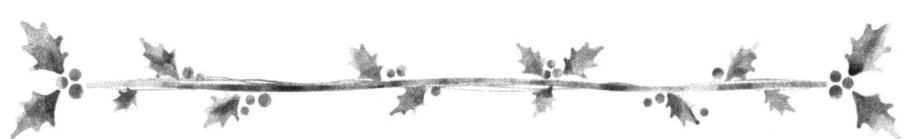

Once Upon a Winter Rest...

Once upon a winter rest, while I gathered sleep and rest,
Over many an ugly and knitted collection of Christmas sweater vests—
    While I thought, tantalizingly thinking, suddenly there came a knocking,
As of some student obtrusively banging, banging at my classroom door.
"Tis some visitor," I yelled, "knocking at my classroom door—
    Whew, only a dream and nothing more."

Chapter Two

Esteem

The Memory Tree

All year long,
Photo albums and scrapbooks provide keepsakes like a family song.

They can be opened at any time
To fill our hearts with treasures so sublime.

However, one time a year,
In a December so near

We bring out a dusty old box from the attic
Containing trinkets of the past so dynamic

To display on a tree –
Live, flocked, green, white, sparkling – one full of glee.

The branches remain as picture hangers like nails,
Always collaged through many years of family tales.

The tourist style from a family vacation
To theme parks or to the capitol of our nation.

The hand painted angel made by a five-year-old daughter with eyes full of spark
In ceramics, while on back, leaving her name as a mark.

That special Santa collectible
Mama couldn't wait to find obtainable.

The very first one given as a gift after marriage
Always hanging as the first one placed from a special box like a carriage.

Whatever the name – Christmas or Holiday – one calls it so.
This tree is a gift each year as the nostalgia continues to grow.

Traditions are passed down to each generation to share
Continuing the Memory tree with love and care.

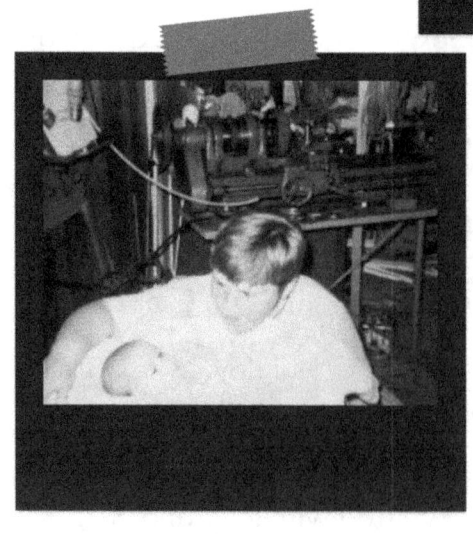

My Brothers Three

When you have siblings, who are brothers and you're the only girl,
Life has a way of sending you in a special kind of whirl.

Especially when you are a generation apart.
Fortunately, for me, they grew in my heart.

As a child, I know I could be a brat,
Tattling on them because we would often spat.

My father nicknamed us a grinch, a grouch, a grump,
and a motormouth from oldest to young.
These three I'm proud to be among.

I always looked up to you three.
At 5, I even skipped school one day to sing songs with glee.

Being at the same school with the youngest one,
He – ten years older than me – I bragged to my classmates a ton.

My oldest I miss every day,
Taken too soon may I say.

Siblings, brothers, how lucky I've been
To have you not only as family, but also as great friends.

February Gal

A wonderful lady born in the cold.
When she arrived that February morn, they broke the mold.

She was Thursday's child and had far to go,
Living a life full of both love and woe.

A nurse by profession was she.
 She cared for everyone, especially her family.

She could embroider, and she loved her books.
As everyone knew; oh, how she could cook!

She was a friend of nature, as a matter of fact.
She truly loved her dogs and cats.

Lapel pins, dolls, and knick-knacks framed her collection.
Pink, the color she loved, complimented her complexion.

Just remember she will always be in you and in me.
She left a multitude of children...a legacy.

A February gal until the very end,
Passing away to the Heavens to visit her old friends.

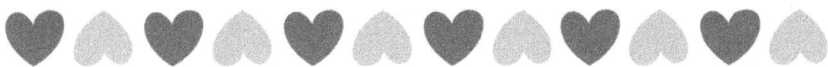

Go Put Your Lipstick On

As a young child,
I never was wild,
Only talked too much.
Upon meeting me, I was mild.

My mother was classy,
Never sassy,
A true June from tv was she
Providing etiquette always to me.

Anytime we would exit the house to leave,
Never a wrinkle on her sleeve,
Her lips were adorned with a rosy hue
I know and believe.

As I got older,
I became bolder
With a hint of a powdery mask on my face
So, I wouldn't look colder.

As a teen,
I would feel I was living the dream
To be with my friends on the scene.
However, my mother would notice
My makeup being lean.

Go put your lipstick on...
She repeated this phrase
With my rolling eye gaze,
But in a haze,
I would do what she says.

Getting into the car,
Not even to go very far,
She would always want me to be a star,

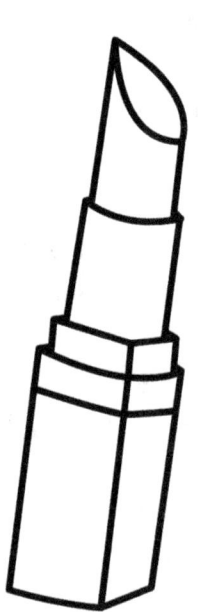

Go put your lipstick on...

Once I lived out and about on my own
Because I thought I was grown,
I would always remember my mother telling me

Go put your lipstick on...

Only a few years later she became ill,
And against her will,
She passed onto something greater still.

When we came into view of her slumbered state,
I wouldn't relate
For many reasons and not believing this was her fate.

Her face had never seemed so colorless,
It seemed like a dream,
Her lips so pale,
Not even a sheen.
I knew there was something that had to be done,
This last one,
I told the man,

Go put her lipstick on...

Until this day,
Twenty-two years since she went away,
Every time I walk out of the house,
I can hear her say,

Go put your lipstick on...

My White Haired Angel

Beautiful hair—a halo of snow white,
Framing her face—a pallor glowing bright.

A soft voice, a sparkling smile—
Crystal blue eyes dancing for miles.

A lady so smart, kindling a kind hear.t
I wish we hadn't lived so far apart.

Always taking time to teach
Skills I would forever keep within my reach.

One task at a time—needlepoint and cross stitch,
Needle arts inspiring my crafting itch.

Only seeing her a few times a year,
Making the most of our time to endear.

My love for cats grew from visiting her own.
Miss Kitty, a sleek Siamese, I'm happy to have known.

Mysteries—we shared a passion!
Agatha Christie who-dun-its were always in fashion.

Reading, a hobby we both had in common,
Encouraging me with a literary love not to be forgotten.

Treating me as a little adult,
Inquisitive conversations would result.

In her last letter to me, she penned,
"I wish I could see you all again."

That wish came true for her and for me, just right.
I hugged her so and she held me so tight.

Almost two decades she has been gone.
I miss her so, leaving me forlorn.

 **Memories with My Dad**

Only having a little more than a decade with a person, especially as a child, makes it hard to remember every detail that made him special as my dad.
Watching space show reruns with him gave me my love of Sci-Fi, which makes me glad.

Only two different times was I to be very quiet: when he was watching football, or napping on the couch after work.
He called me Motor Mouth, so being quiet was difficult much of the time; I was such a dork.

He had his shop to do woodworking, and he loved to work on cars when his time was free,
I tried to stay out of the way so I wouldn't hear "Carmen Marie!"

Movies of vampires, werewolves, and mummies we would watch together staying up late,
As we would have a midnight cheese and cracker snack that was always great!

He would sometimes draw funny cartoon people for me,
As well as play his guitar and sing as I listened with glee.

We would play pool, cards, and dice games,
He went by G. Robert, "Bob," disliking his first name.

Reruns of British spy movies we would watch together, waiting for new ones to come out,
I get my love for the martini drinking spy from my father without a doubt.

Even though I only spent a short time with him before he passed away,
He taught me to be strong, be creative, and be whatever I may.

Uncle Tony

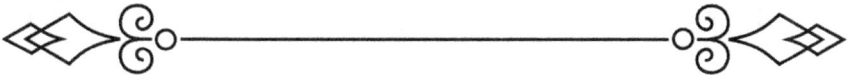

Born in April, a diamond in the rough,
A man's man who was always tough.

A man of honor was he
Serving in the military to help people be free.

He worked an eclectic mix of jobs over the years:
Retail, law enforcement, and fireman with few fears.

A master carpenter was one of his professions,
Crafting beautiful work without any concessions.

He was a talented musician continuously ready to jam
With family and friends always leaving with a finish that would slam.

Referring to everyone as cats and chicks,
When talking to him, it was his schtick.

An animal person we all could ascertain
With his most beloved pet, Burgundy, his Great Dane.

He loved his family, especially the grandkids and Grandma T.
Willing to do anything for her – quality was the key.

Never batting an eye to speak his mind,
Tony was definitely one of a kind.

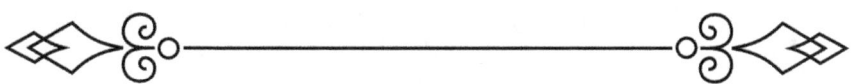

The Giving Season

Every year the season nears
When family and friends find gifts for each other.
Some are funny, some are sweet, and some are sentimental bringing tears,
But some are practical for Father, Mother, and Brother.

Receiving candy, games, and toys
The newest technology so bold
Are the items that are dreamed by girls and boys
Even those who are older might think of trinkets in silver and gold.

Chapter Three

Embrace

The Restless Sea

Darkening mist rolls through waves of sea-worn shores.
Moonlight trickles delicately over of a time of forgotten lore.

The silken, silvery crescent opens wide to accept the passing tide
Only to awaken a longing of a rapturous kiss only two can confide.

The restless sea embraces the two so eagerly entwined as their burning passion mimics the crashing, clashing waves of a tumultuous night.
They achingly yearn for each other's tender caresses with all their delicate soul and willing might.

The exquisite, entrancing beauty of the ocean mirrors the amorous encounter between the two divine,
Igniting a smoldering, never-ending fire ever uniting the blissful two until the end of time.

Vows

When I met you and saw how much we had in common, I knew I wanted to live a long life and prosper with you.

You truly compliment every aspect of who I am as a woman, a nerd, an artist, a music lover, an educator and lifelong learner, a hiker, a pun enthusiast, a television and movie buff, and an adventurer.

When you told me that 3057 was not long enough, you wanted forever, there was no hesitation for me to say yes to be your partner in life, your best friend, and your true love.

I promise to always love, honor, respect, and inspire you every day of our lives, whether it is "the best of times or the worst of times," whether we are healthy or sick, and whether we are rich or poor.

Starting on our marriage trek today, we will embark upon many epic adventures together, where many have yet boldly travelled, laughing and holding hands, walking together side by side into an enchanting life.

As the raven quotes, "Nevermore," shall we be alone, because together, we will "Live! Live the wonderful life that is in us!" to the fullest.

"Tomorrow we will run faster, stretch out our arms farther" to embrace each other with nurture, support, and love. "For our love is a love that is more than love."

I am ready to spend the rest of my days with you; therefore, "Let us Engage!"

Happy Anniversary

One year has passed over time and space,
No one moment would I ever erase.

As I ponder each word I write to you,
My love grows more from every view.

One year represents paper and time,
My gift to you contains my scribe of my rhyme.

Paper doesn't last, but it ignited the flame
To stir the embers to bring us together in one name.

Never-ending time gives us a plethora of adventures to share
Where we will explore and wander whenever we care.

Every morning and every night, I receive kisses times three.
My weirdness you indulge every day for me.

Puns fill our lives at least once a day
As we battle for the best in each one, we say.

We have travelled as many places as we could get
With you ensuring we go to monuments I've always wanted to visit.

One year to the moment we said, "I do,"
I love you even more as each day renews.

Discount Flowers

Arriving home with glee,
My husband with a bouquet to greet me.

Receiving a kiss upon my cheek,
Embracing the flowers, a vase I seek.

With water and food poured in,
I began unwrapping the package with a grin.

As I cut the wrapper
Knowing the stems would be dapper,

I noticed a second sticker on the plastic.
Feeling dread, I knew something might be drastic.

Large and bold DISCOUNT appeared
With bright yellow behind like a roadway sign as I feared.

Some stems were withered and broken.
Disappointment in my eyes must have spoken.

I paused a moment, stepped back to think,
Leaning down pondering at the sink.

Many of the buds were hanging on for life.
If I prune and nurture, I can remove the strife.

Adding every stem and cleaning up the sagging leaves,
Not throwing any of them away, the petals staring at me pleased.

I placed each one ornately in the vase
With care and encouragement, providing a beautiful space.

Joking with my husband about the discount flowers he bought,
I realized something I originally and knowingly had not thought.

This bouquet arrived in my care outside looking shaky,
Realizing very quickly the insides were worth saving.

Once cleaned up showing all their beauty and grace,
I knew never giving up on anything, loving them in their own way was the only case.

Chapter Four

Enrich

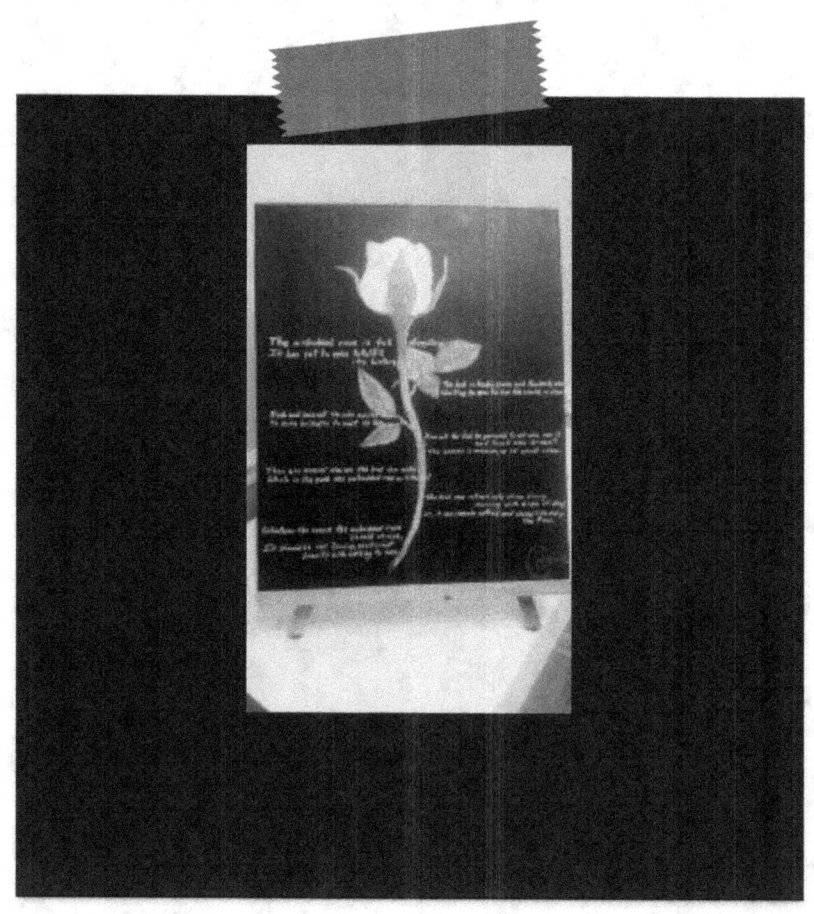

The Unbudded Rose

The unbudded rose is full of mystery.
It has yet to open to fulfill its history.

The bud is freshly green and flawlessly new
Waiting to open to see the world in view.

Fresh and innocent the color awaits
To shine brilliantly to meet its fate.

How will the bud be perceived to all who see it and to all who dream?
The answer is unknown, so it would seem.

There are several choices the bud can make.
Which is the path the unbudded rose will take?

The bud can refreshingly shine every morning with drops of dew.
Or it can remain untried and closed like only the few.

Whatever the course the unbudded rose should choose,
It should be the flowing, exuberant beauty with nothing to lose.

Winding Through Life

Take the positive!
Always be cognitive!

Take the joy!
Always keep happiness employed!

Winding through life
Full of strife

Doesn't need to be dire.
Fill your life with passions laced with fire.

Ascend on an upward spiral
And ignite your amiable attitude to go viral.

Select the Escher path
With unending steps where there is little need for math.

Keep on winding through the stairway of life...
Satisfied, content, and adventurous with a heart that is rife.

Make it So

Through this life, I make this trek
Feeling alone, like a minuscule speck.

I dream of places I hope to see
Brimming with imagination and diversity.

Questions abound with fear of the unknown:
Should I do this? Should I wait to be shown?

Circling around through the neurons in my brain
I ponder the "what ifs" somewhat feeling the strain.

I still ask the question, Should I really go?
In the depths of my mind, I say, "Make it so."

Encountering new people could be scary.
Therefore, I might keep wandering; I will not tarry.

To reach the frontier of mankind, I can hardly wait.
Logic is the only rationale to keep me in a constant state.

I still question; I still hesitate…there is so much to wage…
Should I advance? Should I engage?

This world seems extremely fascinating.
My curiosity peaks…it is scintillating.

I still ask the question, Should I really go?
In the depths of my humanity, I say, "Make it so."

The Scarlet Path

I walk through trees,
I walk through grass,
The time flies by,
It goes so fast.

Searching for the beauty only seen by few,
I wonder if I will find it,
Does it wait for only you?

When one day,
I come upon the scarlet path,
I finally tread upon at last.
My breath its splendor takes
And engulfs me into shuttering in this magnificent place.

Not only does the bloodshot leaves cast a light from the sun,
The crimson roots rise from the earthy ground
Like ruddy, clay tentacles where I saunter upon.
I stare at the wondrous red that spills so perfectly
Like a carpet flowing for the regal ones to stroll.
The spicy, peppery drops of ruby hue create a world of strength for me to extol.

The heat of the scarlet path wraps around me like a warm blanket on a winter's night,
Escaping into rosy depths of peace with utter delight.

A New Paradigm

Every morning is washed anew
With foamy depths of ocean dew.

To gently remove yesterday's unwanted past
To bring forth a tabula rasa alas.

So, the tides carry away the utter calamity of life.
They remove the longing and the endless strife.

Slowly rolling back to the sea
Is the discarded angst and worry of me.

The windswept waves capture those haunted memories holding onto my heart,
Releasing my soul to begin again and seek a brand-new start.

All these hideous thoughts at the bottom of the ocean will stay.
Leaving a fresh perspective, a new paradigm that clings to never going away.

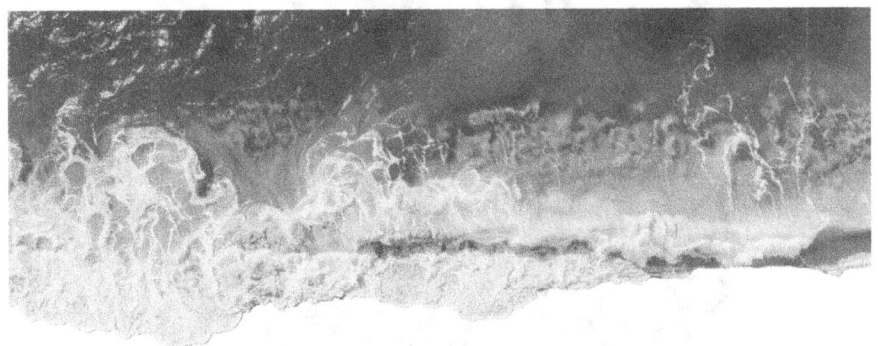

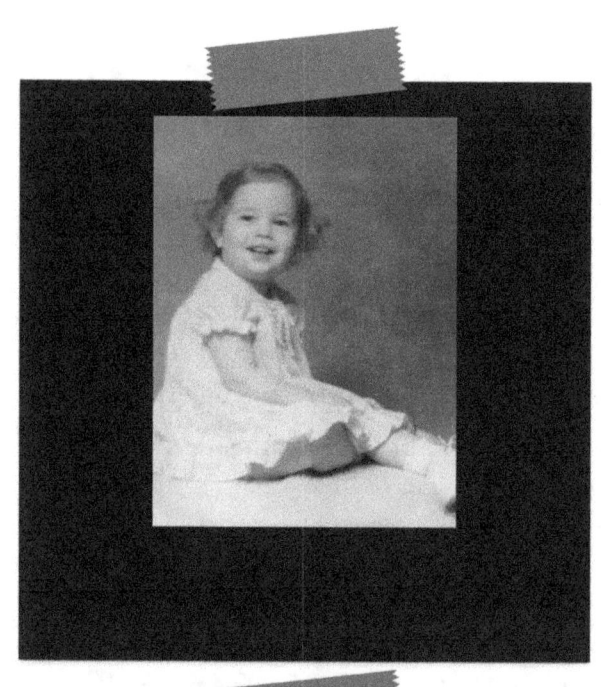

Turning Fifty

It is not a mile marker; it is a milestone.

It is not a corner to turn; it is a crossroads.

It is not kindergarten, or teen angst, or a driver's license, or a first vote, or a first drink, or a rental car, or an age of "something."

It is all those things rolled into one leading up to this point on the path of sidewinding life.

Life is renewed now for something grander than before.

Growing pains have vanished while the lines of wisdom gain momentum with exuberant beauty.

It is a midpoint in this thing we call life counting high towards 100.

Always reaching! Always thinking positive!

It is Tin, atomically speaking, when in its solidified pure state reflects as a mirror seeing the reflection of yourself as "fifty-fifty."

It is golden, a jubilee of life shimmering as the sun rises at dawn.

It is a collection of states, United that is, where every experience in your life happens somewhere, and is tied to a unique, specific place saved in the photo box in your mind.

Vision and hearing seem to begin a slow decline with shiny spectacles and louder volume as accoutrements to enhance the evolved view of the wonderful world mixed with the sagacity and savvy plucked along the way.

Thirty was denial, Forty was scary, Fifty is freedom.

Chapter Five

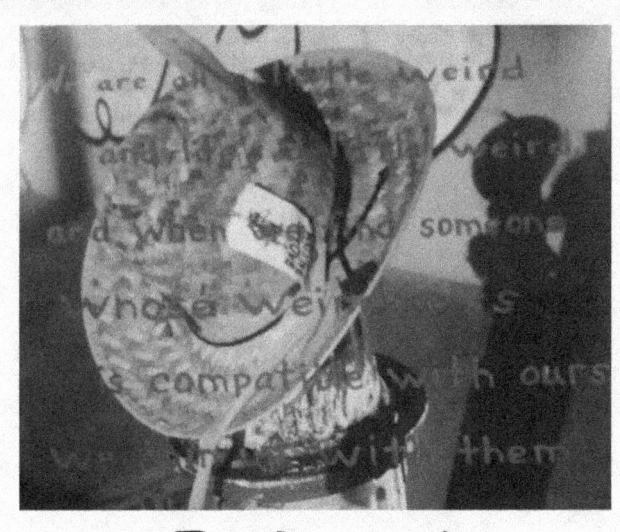

Extend

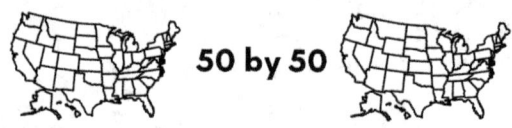

50 by 50

In 1971, a girl from Tennessee came to be
Realizing at a young age, the U. S. she wanted to see.

A few states she must travel through and to
Arkansas to get to Missouri for the family she knew.

Close by was Mississippi, reaching without fret
She would go with Mom and Dad to a clothing outlet.

Still under 10, Alabama and Georgia were reached
When vacationing in Florida at the beach.

Texas was next with family moving in.
Dallas and Houston were travelled to see those kin.

North Carolina, Kansas, Virginia, and Illinois came next
While Kentucky and Indiana were seen on a work trek.

California was always a bucket list state
By way of work, she was able to see how great.

Washington was visited next, the state that is.
At the top of the Space Needle leaving her in a state of dizz.

The bright lights of Las Vegas, Nevada shone so bright
As the desert of Sedona, Arizona with colors of might.

School sent her to a conference in New Orleans, Louisiana after May
Where she experienced the Cajun culture and ate Crawfish Etouffee.

Another state on her bucket list – Hawaii
Fulfilled her dreams of what it would be.

Michigan was attended in a blizzard for a bowl game
While the landscapes of Pennsylvania put many to shame.

Always wanting to visit New York - a dream to see.
While there, she also went over to the state of New Jersey.

Seeing many beaches in her time
She added one more in South Caroline.

Going out west to Colorado made her day,
But walking to the high point of Nebraska, she didn't have much to say.

Mount Rushmore in South Dakota was grand
And Devil's Tower, Ahhh, a place for aliens to land.

Boston, Massachusetts filled with so much colonial history to take in.
Rhode Island and New Hampshire were wonderful day trips to pin.

A world filled with Poe in Baltimore, Maryland
With a jaunt to Delaware - to the beach - not so bland.

Oklahoma, a great state for simplicity and steak,
Travelling quickly to New Mexico for green chilis and hot springs to partake.

Thirty-six complete and fourteen to go
In two years before she turns the big 5-0.

TriStar Traveling

Crossing over the "new" bridge to a different landscape
To a city filled with the blues where I can traipse

Makes me anticipate each place
From the map where I set a path to trace.

My first stop is where the mighty Mississippi rolls on along
As I sit on the cobblestone path I think of many Elvis songs.

The lowlands of the West create a green, flat city on the go
With history of civil rights and Sun Studio.

I get my fill of my childhood haunts,
Then I begin my drive to continue my peaceful jaunt.

My second stop is to the highlands in the middle:
The Capitol, the arts of the Frist, the music of the Ryman, and history where I have nothing to riddle.

The beauty of the city, lakes, and trees on the scene
Continuing traditions never-ending and never lean.

Driving over the Gateway Bridge, the arch's hue continuously changes over the Cumberland River
Makes me sad to leave, but my next spot always delivers.

Arriving at this quaint city so posh and so poetic to the eye,
I walk across the Walnut Street Bridge to the North Shore only to find:

A hamlet filled with exuberant arts and local places to shop
Against the Cumberland River as a peaceful, enchanting back drop.

The mountains of the East are some of the most beautiful I've ever gazed.
My last stop leaves me in a fulfilled, imaginative haze.

This alluring, charming parallelogram of a state
Contains beautiful bridges linking three stars into a triangle as if it were fate.

The lowlands, the highlands, and the mountains provide a plethora of symmetry
Of breathtaking wonder for everyone to experience in its myriad of imagery.

The Urban Playground

Concrete pathways crisscross amongst the cool, green grass
With varieties of trees canvasing like archways for all to pass.

Nestled in a corner where the trees form a shaded tent,
Musicians play from their soul for all to relent.

Shakespeare illuminates the stage with the players on cue
At the bandshell where an abundant audience cannot wait to view.

Lake Watauga, the Sunken Garden, and the Parthenon with their splendor
Remain so breathtaking where people relax, and to their allure, they surrender.

Hidden within the towering buildings of restlessness,
This urban playground offers to all who visit an enchanting oasis.

Whispering, Texting, Walking, & Talking

In the heart of Music City,
An eclectic street concretely exists
Filled with the brightness of lights so pretty,
And music some cannot resist.

Travelers come from everywhere
To visit to and fro
Where they traipse down Broadway as some stare
With copious options, not knowing where to go.

As one watches all who steadily move
Like an assembly line taking a pause for people watching,
Some dress as they feel they have something to prove
As all are whispering, texting, walking, and talking.

The whispers pass between couples and groups
About the interesting and inappropriately dressed.
So not to be overheard, some text pictures of the dupes
To capture outrageous pictorial stories not to be missed.

The path from start to finish is around five blocks
Where walking presents a sensory journey
With food options, honky tonks, and shops
To provide much talking to choose where to be.

This paved path is more beautiful at night
For all who are into gawking
With all the colors of neon lights
As all are whispering, texting, walking, and talking.

 **Traveling the Electronic Christmas Highway**

Let's take an electronic roadway trip to enjoy
Through several cities bringing Christmas joy!

Meet Me in St. Louis back in time for the World's Fair of 1904,
While we rode the trolley to meet the boy next door.

From there, we will drive to Chicago, Illinois to the suburbs of one Griswold family,
Where we will help solve the problem of Christmas lighting, so ALL can see.

We travel next to New York City where Macy's on 34th Street is host
To a real Santa who always brings the most.

In addition, a lady and her daughter are always feeling blue
And Kris Kringle restores their attitude with *"Faith is believing when common sense tells you not to."**

We stay in the city and visit the Bishop and The Bishop's Wife
Where we meet the angel, Dudley, who helps everyone remember the big picture of life.

On we go to see George Bailey and another angel, Clarence, in Bedford Falls
Where Clarence helps George realize It's a Wonderful Life no matter the worst of it all.

We move on to some singing and dancing with Bing and the crew
At Holiday Inn in Midville, Connecticut only open for certain holidays of the few.

**Credited to the film, Miracle on 34th Street.*

We remain in this state and end up on Elizabeth Lane's enchanting, magazine ready farm,
Where we are hoping for a Christmas in Connecticut with all the glee and charm.

We arrive in technicolor at Columbia Inn in Pine Tree, Vermont to finish out our traveling list,
Surprisingly, there is no snow, only to be enchanted on the 25th with a White Christmas.

There is so much to glean from these movies of old,
Love your family and friends without being told.

Taking this electronic journey is a feat, both great, and not small!
Please take it sometime, and Merry Christmas to one and to all!

Land of Enchantment

Enchantment

Only begins to describe the

Resounding

Beauty of this land.

Landscapes resemble

Shape shifters

Morphing from a glorious prairie

To a sandy desert in an instant where tumble weeds

Frolic

Into gardens of yucca, cholla, and prickly pears

For miles and miles to the eye's delight.

Lakes and rivers fulfill the role of

Mirrors

To reflect the incredible mountain-scapes

Encompassing

This vast spread of magnificence.

The Rio Grande

Concurrently

Displays itself in many cities, so one doesn't forget its

Splendor

To the sustenance of the land.

The hot springs of Truth or Consequences

Engulfs

Its partakers with the natural warmth

And minerals to sufficiently sooth the soul.

Basalt lava flow

Blankets

The Valley of Fire in a never-ending sea

Of the midnight hue of the witching hour visibly

Contrasting

The cascading rocks against the shrubbery

With the native desert plants.

The Land of Enchantment

Summons

All who visit to repeatedly return

To the unexpected charm of the

Southwest.

NYC Sounds

In the early minutes of morning twilight,
There is a certain quiet that lingers.
In the distance, you can just hear
The subway's wheels screech
Like an owl landing on its prey.

As the dawn breaks,
The hustle and bustle of heartbeats
Move throughout the city -
 Getting to coffee shops
 Getting to work
 Getting to school

Moving to and fro,
Meeting deadlines.
Tourists add to the foot pounding beat on the pavement.
The noises of walking, running, traffic, and talking loiter
Into the twilight of the evening just before dusk.

In places like Times Square,
The buildings come alive
As the lights switch on
Around 42nd Street and Broadway.

Even in Central Park,
The rhythmic patterns exist
With the squirrels frolicking,
Pigeons cooing,
The hot dog vendors selling,
The skaters at the rink swishing,
And organ music of the carousel
Adds a whimsical childlike tune of yesteryear.

The sounds of people never stop,
Repeating over and over,
A similar song from day to day...
Except for that brief period of the morning before dawn.

Minnesota: Land of 10,000 Lakes

Driving through Minnesota,
So much water to see.
So many shades of blues and greens,
Coloring the world around me.

Trees form the landscape:
Balsam Firs, Tamaracks, and Black Spruce.
The White Spruce almost blue in color,
And the Eastern Hemlock belongs in Dr. Seuss.

The beaches provide picnic areas for the day.
Around Lake Minnetonka, marshes surround,
As the people boat and bike
In Excelsior, a quaint little town.

Minneapolis, so people friendly
With bike lanes and walking paths galore.
Sitting amongst the remnants of the past
With industrial flour ruins from a time before.

While walking through the tree umbrellaed streets,
The twin, St. Paul, even more in keeping of the past.
Neighborhoods from a time of Gatsby
Where a faint jazz note seems to last.

Minnesota, Minnesota,
A state unable to disappoint and fulfill dreams.
The natural beauty calling me back
Because you are much more than you seem.

This is West Virginia

Driving the highway

From Maryland

All around

Seeing lovely

Shades of green:

Fern, forest, pine.

Rolling hills of green,

Hints of blue

From the sunlight,

Bouncing off the leaves.

Stopping in history,

Harper's Ferry,

Blanketed by flowing waters

The confluence –

The Shenandoah and the Potomac.

Sacred ground

To honor those who died

From that raid

Long ago.

A quaint town,

Preserved.

A state...

Picturesque...

This is West Virginia...

Party on Wheels

Desiring a streetcar to arrive as soon as it can,
Heading back to the quarter was the plan.

Sitting outside a café admiring the houses of the district garden,
We heard some loud music while talking where I had to say, "Pardon."

Coming down the street was a tiny carriagelike vehicle with pedals
Sporting a surrey on top decked out in black drape with silver accents of metal.

An adult size tricycle we all saw when it glided into sight
Bearing a biblical quote, "Judge not that you be not judged," in all caps full of might.

A little lady with an autumn physique and a spring mind was peddling without hesitation
And smiling so gleefully to bring us her mobile entertainment station.

Adorned in red fringe draping her frame
With sandals and Cleopatra headdress in shiny, sparkling silver to name.

She stood up on her pedals and shook to and fro
As she smiled and blew kisses as she would to a beau.

We waved and we wooed as she passed us by onto her next stop
Seeing the back end of her carriage with "Party on Wheels" like she had just done a mic drop.

When in New Orleans, you never know what you will see
As we go on treks down different streets awaiting some kind of mystery.

The very next day as we took a leisurely stop to eat beignets,
We heard that loud music that almost put us in a daze.

"Party on Wheels" appeared again right outside the patio gate
She stopped and danced in her gold and purple as if in a Mardi Gras state.

We all blew her a kiss as she reciprocated back
Leaving us entertained in sheer delight with nothing to lack.

Not sure if we would ever see her again,
Later that night she was dancing on Bourbon recognizing us as if we were close friends.

"Party on Wheels" left such an impression
Her name remains a mystery leaving her as a living legend.

 **Summer Escape to Firefly Cottages**

From the road, all you see are bright colored hues,
Peeking through the trees with a brick walkway to pursue.

Stepping across the threshold of anticipated dreams
Is an abode from the outside more than it seems.

Nine cottages, not all in symmetrical rows,
Nestled around an enchanting paradise where beautiful plants flow.

Each bungalow styled in its own unique charm and grace,
Keeping true to its 1950s quaintness and "swell" space.

The communal den, centered around an old live oak,
Wrapped in twinkling lights welcoming all of us folk.

Lounging at the shoreline any part of the day,
Watching rosette spoonbills and gulls leave you breathless with not much to say.

Each day, the tide ebbs and flows to reveal
Mud flats, salt marshes, and oyster bars for you to see with zeal.

The breeze caresses the nook, especially in the shade,
Bringing the salty smell of the ocean while the little lizards are at play.

Dragon flies buzzing all around
While the small fiddler crabs at the water's edge to their holes scurry down.

Nostalgic, but timeless, Firefly Cottages in Cedar Key provide to the soul
As each visitor stays for their own designed purpose and goal.

The Watery Dance in Key Largo

Dancing waters play a continuous tune,
Washing away each day's rays waiting for the moon.

Seas so clean like looking through a thin piece of glass,
Rocks and sandy floors seen eyes pass.

To and fro the waves "cha cha" as they crest,
Some larger, seeming like bigger steps giving it zest.

Peeking into the aquatic world through goggling glasses like a window,
Seeing coral, shells, fish, and an occasional barracuda on the go.

Other creatures creep in this deep –
Jelly fish, nurse sharks, and manatees sometimes even peep.

The sea is their dance floor
As humans and birds look on from the shore.

Peaceful music kept on repeat
Leaving the watery bliss always available on beat.

Don't Skimp the Mint

Oh, to the happy green plant used each day
To garnish tiki cocktails, works of art I must say.

A leaf, a sprig, or a stem are too few.
A bunch or a handful only will do.

> When the cocktail is shaken from the heart of a gent,
> Grab a bundle and smack it, and don't skimp the mint.

Cultivated by the Egyptians around 3,000 years ago.
Embraced by Vic and Don, tiki guys we all know.

Aromatic sweetness, cool and strong,
Square stems branching lanceolated leaves, one can't go wrong.

> When the cocktail is shaken from the heart of a gent.
> Grab a bundle and smack it, and don't skimp the mint.

Special spirits and juices are mixed
Receiving stems smoothly slid into ice pebbles betwixt.

The glass with fruit is garnished,
And finally, the swizzle is swished.

> When the cocktail is shaken from the heart of a gent.
> Grab a bundle and smack it, and don't skimp the mint.

Chapter Six

Endure

Why did you leave me all alone?

Why did you leave me all alone?
You never knew me when I was grown.
I know it was not your fault; how could you have known?

You were in my life only in the blink of an eye.
I wish I could have learned more from you before the time went by.
Till this day, I still question and wonder why.

I can only ponder if you were just meant to be here for a short while.
In that short time frame, you always made me smile.
I commit to memory certain attributes for life to file.

What I gained from you is a wealth of knowledge you imparted on me
From observations, stories, and actions I gained for free.
Keeping your values from what I gathered was always the key.

You taught me to work hard and never give up on my dreams,
To believe in myself because I am the only one to make my light beam,
To keep learning and doing to keep my mind gathering information to glean.

The Unsettled Soul

The whispering wind calms the unsettled soul
With a promise of tomorrow and fettered feelings under control.

Each glorious day moves in time and space
Never knowing which pieces of life will be replaced.

Nights sweep through, creeping darker as dusk twirls in,
Rousing up destined dreams causing the mind to sagaciously spin.

Decisive dawn wakes the soul anew,
Bringing forth the rebirth of the morn with life's answers ringing true.

The Seminal Sea

Oh, what thrashing waters crash down with no repent.
Long are the dogged days ceaselessly spent
Waiting for whispering words to be truly answered with no relent,
Windswept hopes wonderfully wrapped up in timeless tides from a gallant gent.

The seminal sea holds the mystical message – what is groundbreakingly and sincerely meant.
Will the white capped, thundering waves find peace to be sent?
Only the precious patience of the longing love may assent
As she hungrily awaits for the riotous wind to painlessly die away and finally provide her with serene content.

 **Shrill Cry for a Forlorn Love**

As the golden arcs of oats gleamed bright,
The sun awakened from an endless night.

The sweeping tide devastatingly washed away all intended paths,
Only to reveal the shiny, sun-kissed shells having baths.

She rises up from a cold, dark, wet slumbering bed,
Only to reveal her dire secrets and still to be filled with dread.

Love everlasting is her desire alas,
But her doomed fate has already been unfortunately cast.

High-pitched shrills of angelic streams of patterned notes cry
For her true love to longingly hear, to hurriedly find her, and to release his sigh.

She uncontrollably beckons forth for her dashing mate,
Little does he know of his untimely fate.

Displaced

Does a school have a heart?
Does it reside without people only in part?

Is it more like a ribcage surrounding the beating muscle?
Or do the teachers pump the energy in and out as they hustle and bustle?

Brick and mortar prolong the life by standing tall.
However, the little ones ignite life by flowing through the halls.

Two months have passed, almost three
Of missing beautiful smiles and minds of wonderment and glee.

Distance will finally come and go,
Holding on to wait until the world says so.

A building is just an empty shell with a face.
Right now, its heart is only temporarily displaced.

Connections

In this time of separation,
Remember the intention.
Especially now, there is no time for rejection.
Hold onto your connections!

Connections are now different than before.
They take place behind a closed door.
Away from the maddening crowd of our yore
Voice and virtual command our communication floor.

These times should make you appreciate
Everyone to whom you relate
Whether by blood or fate.
Cling to your connections beyond the expiration date...

Of our locked in world right now and here.
This is only temporary, so please persevere.
Situations are dynamic and eventually move behind us somewhere,
But your connections are static, always needing your care.

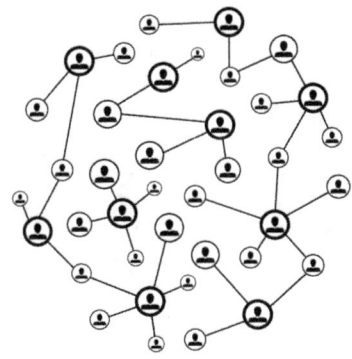

Chapter Seven

Exist

Ode to Coffee

O sweet elixir of the morning,

You call to my olfactory sense through the wafts of robust fragrance stunning my being.

I am in a trance until the hot, bitter liquid touches my lips

To awaken me from my sleeping lair.

My mind contains a fog until several ounces have coursed through my veins

To create an alertness to the day.

O coffee, O coffee, you remain my forever companion through life

To ease me through each impending day,

And to keep me revived as I courageously battle each daunting task I face.

Longing for Spring

Peering out the open window
To the cold, damp grounds of winter,
Our hearts ache and feel low.

The sky's canvas painted in matte, grayish hues
Serves as the backdrop of a winter's day
Slowly gathering crystalized flakes of dew.

As the calendar moves closer to March,
The perennials ache to push through the soaked soil
From all of winter's replenishing,
leaving nothing parched.

We anticipate the bright, fresh hint of green
Peeking out ready for the sun's splendor,
As we long for spring to persistently be seen.

Ode to Spring

On a cold February morning, overcast and solemn, looking out my rear window brings me joy as the daffodils peek through the soil eyeing the coming sun of March.

I long for the crisp winds sweeping in the rush of spring.

Oh Spring, how we delight and celebrate your name!

You renew our faith winter is complete, and solitude is over, bringing forth the beautiful, shiny carpet of elegant green to skip lightly on the path towards fulfillment of flowers to calm our deficient soul.

Oh Spring, we welcome you like the wayward friend returning home carrying bouquets of brightly colored flowers to ask forgiveness for being gone so long.

Oh Spring, please color our fields in fertile wonder filled with an artist's palette of superb beauty waiting to be painted on the canvas of life.

Daisies

Snow white petals spring forth with glee
Around a sunshine center awaiting a bee.

They can be wild; they can be free.
They can be planted in a pot under a tree.

Wisping in the wind as if right on key
As the evergreen leaves mimic the music only for me.

They always are friendly; they always are lively.
They always welcome everyone smiling and happy.

Daisies caress my hand as I bend on one knee
As I look out into the meadow – a field of amity and beauty do I see.

The Pink Gardenia

The pink gardenia:
Is there such a thing?
Of man or myth
From whence did it spring?

A bloom of blush
So fair and pure
Did you really see one?
Are you really sure?

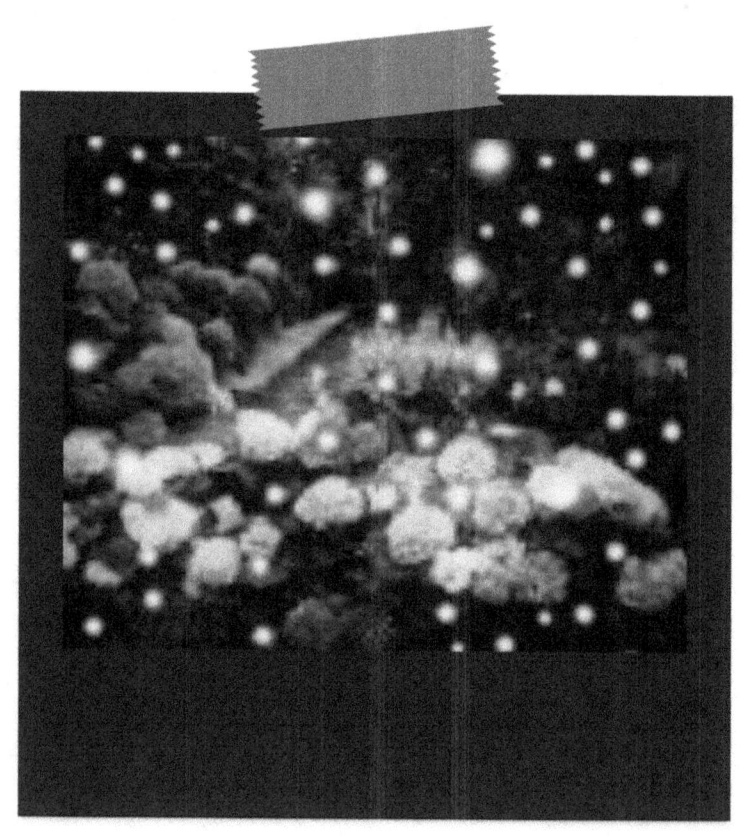

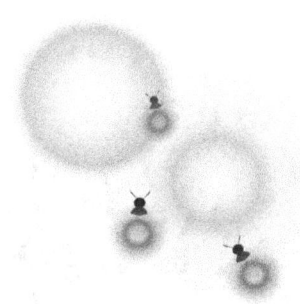

Fireflies

Firefly, firefly ray of light
Don't leave me alone
Guide me through the night.

Your light is shown
To give me sight.

Firefly, firefly ray of light
Show me the way,
Please don't take flight.

Will it be Fire, or Will it be Ice?

Some Houses stand strong.
Some Houses stand divided.
We're waiting for the last song.
What will be decided?

Many standing high,
Looking for the victory.
The end is nigh...
Has the season been too wintery?

Each battle is dire!
Who wins or dies is a roll of the dice.
Who belongs to fire?
And who belongs to ice?

Armies have fought.
Dragons have blazed.
One dagger brought
The Night King's last days.

Now, the Lion is one,
The Dragon is almost two,
The Wolves are almost four, except for one son
Who pledges his allegiance to a Queen he thought he knew.

What alliances will hold?
What betrayals will ensue?
Will madness be bold?
Or will intelligence win for a few?

Who belongs to fire?
Who belongs to ice?
It is the man who is no liar
Blended with both flames and bitter cold who has lived twice.

Light has come for those who knew.
Darkness has come for some.
In the end, we know who will prevail for you.
Those from the House where winter has come.

ABOUT THE AUTHOR

Carmen Bouldin

Carmen Bouldin works as an English teacher. She has worked in education since 2004. In her spare time, she writes gothic romance, mystery, and poetry. Much of her writing and art is inspired by Edgar Allan Poe. Her debut novella, *The Rose Bush*, was published in 2025. Her poem, "The Raven's Mourning," was nominated for a Saturday Visiter Award in 2020. This poem was also published in Raven's Quoth Press' poetry anthology, Evermore, in 2024. She also cohosts a podcast, The Six Degrees of Edgar A. Poe, where she and her POEcast partner, Jeanie Smith, discuss Poe's influences on multiple genres. She also enjoys creating visual art. Her painting, "There's no Place like Poe," was nominated for a Saturday Visiter Award in 2019. A native Memphian, Carmen resides in Middle Tennessee with her husband, Jeff, and their black cat, Poe. Carmen and Jeff love to travel and wear vintage inspired attire Carmen creates through the art of sewing.

You may find Carmen's writing, art, and sewing at the following:

Website: https://thequotableraven.com/

Facebook - @thequotableraven

X - @thequoteraven

Instagram -

    Writing: @thequoteableraven

    Sewing: @ravenmade23

You may find Carmen and Jeanie's POEcast at:

Website: www.sixdegreesofpoe.com

Facebook – @the6degreesofedgarallanpoe

X – @sixdegreesofpoe

Instagram – @sixdegreesofpoe

Spotify – The 6 Degrees of Edgar Allan Poe

YouTube – https://www.youtube.com/@poeunplugged3978

www.ingramcontent.com/pod-product-compliance
Lightning Source LLC
Chambersburg PA
CBHW072116050526
44107CB00098BA/268